WE ARE FAMILY

AND THIS IS MY STORY

I0620660

He was raised by a single parent, he overcame
the limitations of childhood poverty and has
been battling Parkinson's Disease
for twenty-five years.

RYAN KELLEY, ED.D.

Chapbook Press

Schuler Books
2660 28th Street SE
Grand Rapids, MI 49512
(616) 942-7330
www.schulerbooks.com

We Are Family, And This is my Story

ISBN 13: 9781966196112

Library of Congress Control Number: 2024926588

Printed in the United States.

"Sometimes when bad things happen to good people, people can sour...this has not happened to Ryan Kelley. We have known Ryan long before his Parkinson's diagnosis, his positive attitude toward life has never faltered. As you read about his life, the love shared in his home is evident. As Ryan discloses his humble beginnings to us, which in itself is courageous, we may be given a clue as to how he has overcome life's many challenges. Ryan shares many humorous anecdotes about students, friends, and family. Humor, positivity and an undertone of genuine caring for others is evident throughout this book. Ryan's ability to stay positive in the face of obstacles should be a true inspiration to us all to stay positive and to spread love to the world."

—Chris and Pam Wise
(friend and retired school teacher, respectively)

"Dr. Ryan Kelley worked for the Rockford Public School district for over 30 years. I was blessed to call him my principal. As a teacher under his leadership, I looked forward to staff meetings. He filled every moment with humorous stories, life experiences, and funny details about his family. Time spent with Ryan was joyous and memorable. This must-read book showcases his life journeys and upbringing in a comedic and memorable style. His struggles with Parkinson's also depicts his courage. We all applaud Dr. Ryan Kelley."

—Colleen Pierson, GVSU Professor

Contents

Acknowledgments

Thank you to all of the people who helped me share my story by providing encouragement, giving honest feedback, and proofreading. Special thanks to Jeff Bryant, Chris Wise, Pam Wise, Ty Kelley, Bryce Kelley, Reid Kelley, Jody Kelley, Brian Tierney, Heidi Tierney, Neil Blakeslee and Dan Royer. Also, thank you to all of my immediate family members, as well as my extended family members for their support and interest.

Introduction

There are many reasons for writing my life story. First, it has been a very interesting life, filled with ups and downs. I have tried to capture many of the memories of my 31-year career as a public school teacher and administrator. Another reason is to share all that I have learned while battling Parkinson's Disease over the past twenty-five years. Additionally, I want to keep my promise to all the people who told me, "You better be writing these stories down and make a book after you retire." I also hope that I can make use of my first-hand experience with living in poverty. Mostly, I want the readers to enjoy the stories of my life, and to accept that "Life is Good," and they need to "Live, Love, and be Grateful," every day! There are so many people who do not appreciate their good health and good friends until they are taken away. Make the most of every day.

I have titled this book *We Are Family*. As I reflect on my life, it has not been all rainbows and unicorns. It has been filled with opportunities to overcome obstacles. Included in the list of obstacles are the following:

- Being raised by a single parent
- Growing up in poverty
- Diagnosed with Parkinson's at the age of 34

Reflecting on the past, there is more than enough material and information to fill a book. On a daily basis, at our homes and at our schools, interesting things were taking place. For example, we did not have a car, there was no running water, and there were very few clothes. Our house could best be described as being unsanitary. An example of this is our mom bringing in a pregnant goat to give birth on the living room floor. I believe the stories shared will surprise you and will remain in your memories for a long time.

In addition to entertaining readers, I want to share some ideas and strategies on how to overcome the challenges that families are facing. Despite the unusual circumstances, we were lucky to be able to stay together as a family and not be divided up by social services and placed in foster care. Lastly, at the age of 34, I was diagnosed with Parkinson's Disease. I am the only person in our immediate family with this disease. We are family!

An additional purpose in writing this book is to create a document that can be shared with future generations of Kelleys, and to share our life story. Also, it may motivate other families to overcome obstacles that they are facing, and perhaps write their own story. Regardless, I hope it benefits everyone who reads it. The stories are 100% true.

Life is Good!
Live, Love, and be Grateful.

Chapter 1—My Family

*Annabel, the goat was ready to give
birth when my mom said: "Bring
Annabel inside into the living room
where it is warmer."*

My mom, Marcia Gould, was a person committed to making the world a better place. However, she understood that her first responsibility was to meet the demands of the difficult job of raising five kids, with relatively little support. She took on the many added duties of being a single parent, because she thought in the long run it would give her kids a better life. So, given the personal differences that existed between my mom and dad, and the many differences in perspectives with the Women's Rights Movement, they got a divorce. My mom took the kids to Shingleton, Michigan in the Upper Peninsula, where she had a friend named Lucia Wolf. What ultimately resulted was all five of us kids graduating from high school and furthering our education beyond high school. Four of us earned bachelor's degrees. We went on to have successful careers in the following professions/ positions: teachers, administrators, medical doctor, truck driver, structural engineer, business owner, and social worker. This was very uncommon for our neighborhood in Shingleton, as many of the young adults were content to work at the lumber yard, papermill, or at a prison, which I respect.

We attended school in Munising and felt that we received a great education. Our success in school didn't happen by accident. It was instilled in us, that we would work diligently and we would be successful in college.

Athletics played a significant role in our commitment to school. We had some great varsity coaches, including Coach Terry Sayen (football), Coach Jim Landfair (basketball), Coach Joe Hayes (basketball), Coach Don Hudon (summer baseball) and Coach Fran DesArmo (track and field). Coach Landfair was my mentor for many years!

———————————

My mom was one of a kind. They broke the mold after creating her. She always saw things in a different frame of light. There are many examples of this unusual behavior, here are two:

- First, she got into a fist fight with the neighbor lady. She could not remember why she got into a fight This was unusual behavior for my mom because she always stressed nonviolent solutions.

- A second example of her unique behavior was at wedding receptions. She would be the only person on the dance floor. Her eyes were closed and her lips were pointed out—she was in her own world.

An interesting fact about my mom and dad is they were the homecoming king and the queen at Union High School in Grand Rapids, Michigan in 1955. I'm sure they looked like the perfect couple. So, they got married at a young age and had four children in four years. They waited an additional three years to have child number five, me.

Sovereign Couple Rule Over "55" Homecoming

Sparkling Marcia Flathof and Handsome Bob Kelley were crowned by Principal Robert Stark, King and Queen of Union's Homecoming, November 5, 1954, at Houseman Field. Reigning with them at the Homecoming Dance held in the Dillingham Gym after the game, were their attending court members. Left to right are, Nancy Allgood, Inky Olive, King Bob Kelley, Queen Marcia Flathof, Dorothy De Wys, and Pat Soulis. Also in the court were Ron Feenstra, Dick Green, Mel Visser, and Gary Hoff.

As mentioned, mom raised five kids, without any assistance—(actually, she had six kids, but the oldest son, Pat, did not think the Yooper lifestyle agreed with him. So, he moved back to Grand Rapids to live with our dad). We were very proud of our mom. We loved and respected her. We never had a big house, or the fine clothes, or expensive cars. Mom would always tell us, "More important than material things, we have each other"—that is so true! We are family!

Growing up in the Upper Peninsula of Michigan, there were many strange things that occurred that we were not prepared for. An example of this is how we did not have enough food, so we ate whatever was available to survive. We also needed to learn new cultural norms, such as putting the seat down in the outhouse. This would have prevented our dog from falling down the outhouse hole and my brother, Sean from being hung by his feet, upside down, to get the dog out of the hole.

We also joked with mom about some of her quirks. She was okay with us laughing about her behavior, so long as we were not disrespectful and never hurtful. We teased her that she thought that because she gave birth to six kids, she deserved some sort of award, like a free parking pass or get out of jail free card. At least a few times a day, she would break wind. Of course, we would complain about the odor, to which she would respond, "If you gave birth to six kids, you would have gas problems, too." Another thing she complained about, was the appearance of varicose veins. I can still hear her say, "You try giving birth to six kids with big heads. You would have varicose veins on your legs, too."

Another family memory that we talk about is the annual Thanksgiving Day drive from Shingleton to Grand Rapids, to visit our grandparents and uncles. MapQuest had the average travel time as 5 hours and 29 minutes, but it took us 13 hours and 30 minutes. Everyone got there safely, but there was always a level of danger when we drove the old truck with the camper attached to the back. The truck was getting near the end of its life. The odometer broke at about 250,000 miles, and while seated inside the truck you could look down and see the yellow lines on the road through the floorboards. Many times, when in the camper, the door would blow open and we would be too scared to shut it, afraid we would fall out. As cars passed us by, the people were waving at mom, trying to get her attention to let her know the kids are not safe in the camper. Mom simply waved back at them and said "there are a lot of friendly people in the U.P."

Another thing about our Thanksgiving trip was the increase in our vocabulary. Whenever something went wrong with the truck, or when another car was laying on the horn because we were traveling at 35 miles per hour in a 65 miles per hour speed zone, mom would shout out words that were not very nice. She did not respond with an "oh shoot," or a "crap," or even a "damned it." Rather, at the top of her lungs she would shout "F--- A DUCK!"

We all looked forward to Thanksgiving—we are family. Another event we all enjoyed was the Munising High School commencement ceremony. As each of us kids graduated from high school, we had a party to celebrate. We would see the same relatives that we saw at Thanksgiving, including Grandpa and Grandma Palecki, Great Grandma Stewart, Jack Palecki, Uncle Craig and Uncle Jack.

Everybody looked up to my mom's younger brother, Jack, who earned his doctoral degree in chemical engineering at Ohio State University and lives in Santa Barbara, California. For anybody who needed a mentor, Uncle Jack made himself available.

At the graduation parties, instead of everyone drinking coffee and pop, everyone was drinking beer from a keg. Grandma Palecki always warned Grandpa that if he got drunk at the party, on the drive home, they would be stopping at every gift shop between Shingleton and Grand Rapids. Her threats never seemed to bother Grandpa; he just kept on drinking. Also, who could forget Uncle Craig pumping the keg.

Great Grandma Stewart was about 90 years old when she took her final trip to watch her great granddaughter graduate from high school. Great grandma rode to the U.P. with Grandma Palecki and needed assistance with most activities. One night she stayed at our house. It must have been about 3:00 AM and we were all awakened by her screaming, "Where are the towels? I'm stuck to the toilet seat and the water won't stop overflowing. I need some towels." It was cold, the bed was comfy, and nobody wanted to get out of bed. The water was getting into the boys' bedroom, coming from under the wall. So, we picked up our shoes and placed them on top of the bed and fell back asleep. This was not a highlight of our childhood. We felt bad, and our mom was disappointed in us. She wanted us to always help those who could not help themselves.

Mom valued education, referring to it as the great equalizer! With a quality education, you can become anything you want to be. She expected her kids to further their education beyond high school and she kept a close eye on our grades—she had high expectations. She started out every report card meeting the same way, "Well Ryan, I see you have five "A's and one "A-". Why are you struggling so much in the A-minus class?"

Growing up in Shingleton, Michigan, population about 400, it's safe to say that we chose the path less traveled. Thinking back, things were pretty rough. Our morning routine, in the winter, included one of us kids building a fire in the wood stove, taking a pot from the kitchen and going outside and filling it with snow, putting the pot on the woodstove to melt the snow, using the water from the melted snow to prime the outdoor pump then filling up some containers for the rest of the day. Another step in process, whenever we ran out of firewood, was getting up early on Saturdays and Sundays and cutting down some trees for firewood. Mom always said that firewood needed to "season" for 6 months before burning. "Green" firewood was not safe and it did not burn very well either. Mom always used the power chain saw to cut down the trees. Once on the ground, branches were removed and cut into pieces that would fit in the woodstove. The trunks of the larger trees were usually too large and needed to be split with an axe before usage.

Another change to our daily routines was our diet and eating habits. I don't remember ever eating red meat, with one exception. I remembered that mom prepared a huge meal for us that night. She said the meat came from the neighbor man down the road, who shot a deer and gave some of the meat to us. In the morning, when we were providing water to all of the animals, we found out that our pet goat, named Paint, must have broken free from his rope. Mom said he must have gotten scared during the thunder and lightning storm. It was several years later when mom told us the truth about that meal. As we put our heads together, the clues to this case of the missing goat led us to believe that maybe the goat did not run away— mom did not even have us look for Paint the next morning. So, we asked mom if we ate our pet goat, Paint. She confirmed that we indeed ate Paint—we are family?

Much of the food we ate was seasonal. In the summer we would go fishing, mainly wading the Hickey Creek for brook trout. Also, in the summer we would go berry picking and we would always get apples off the trees. In the winter we would hunt rabbits and, in the fall, we went after partridge and also went smelt dipping.

Some other "meals" included gravy, poured over bread (the gravy was made using Cream of Wheat.) Peanut butter sandwiches were a popular food item. Mom would buy ten pound mini-barrels of peanut butter from the food co-op. When we opened the barrel, there was about an inch or two of oil resting on top. The first person to use it was supposed to stir it up, so the entire tub was creamy and easy to spread. However, it never worked out that way. Usually, the last few pounds of peanut butter were very dry and when we would try to spread it over the bread it would tear apart the sandwich.

I do remember mom cooking and frequently substituting ingredients. Rarely would she have a complete set of ingredients for the recipe. I remember her making chicken noodle soup, without chicken. Another example of alternative food items that we ate were leeks—they taste like onions, but are smaller. The problem with the leeks was the goats would eat them, causing the goat's milk to taste terrible. Other alternatives include using mayonnaise in place of eggs, and honey in place of sugar. One other food item that can be found in every Yooper's kitchen is Trenary Toast. Trenary Toast is as hard as a brick and it has a half-life of about 100 years.

Finding clothes to wear was also an experience. Being the youngest boy, I received hand-me-downs. I remember clothes shopping at second-hand stores like St. Vincent DePaul. I remember playing Little League baseball in leather work boots, because my shoes fell apart. The two terms used in our house were, "hand-me-downs" and "grow into." A good example of this is the sweater I received as a Christmas gift when I was in 7th grade. I finally grew into it just in time for my senior picture.

My "grow into" sweater—senior picture

Regardless of where we purchased our clothing, mom would not want us to lose any clothes. So, she would take a permanent marker and write our name on everything. For example, I bought an orange hunting hat with the unsnap and pull-down ear covering. My mom wrote my name on it from ear to ear. It was large enough for airplanes to read.

Looking back on all of these stories, many involve our mom's strange behavior. She showed up unannounced at our front door in Rockford, Michigan, in the middle of the night, 350 miles away from her home. I think the only person more surprised than us was her husband who woke up in an empty bed back in the U.P. Looking back, these were signs of her bi-polar condition.

Another example of bizarre behavior from my mom was her announcement that she was voting for Donald Trump. I'm not going to write about politics, but it was big news. This surprised many, as she has been very critical of the candidate's conservative political party. She has always been involved in the political process. As a matter of fact, her strong and passionate feelings towards the Women's Rights Movement, was the primary reason for mom and dad's divorce. Each had strong feelings and nobody would bend.

Mom was a pretty good athlete and she enjoyed playing softball. She always hit the ball very hard and would always slide head-first into second base—even if there wasn't a play at second base. As she was well aware, her blue jeans/softball pants had a broken zipper and she always fixed it with about five safety pins. However, the safety pins could not match the force of a head first slide. So, after each head first slide, every player on both teams would help try to find the scattered pins.

Another memory I have of my mom is during high school sporting events. During the key parts of the game, we could hear her yelling "it's time to get tough," sometimes followed by a "wooohooo!" When the Northern Michigan University football coaches came to our house to offer me a full ride scholarship, mom felt the urge to demonstrate her talent. Everybody had a good laugh. Even today, when faced with difficult situations, Parkinson's or otherwise, I can hear her voice hollering "get tough wooohooo!"

Mom was many things to many people. Topping the list, she was a Christian, a mother, a daughter, a friend, a county commissioner, an aunt, a cousin, an author, an artist and many others. To some, she was a dreamer. To others she was the homecoming queen and to many she was the writer of many letters to the editor in the local newspapers. She knew that she could do a better job in local leadership positions, so she ran an election campaign and won. She was very proud to serve as an Alger County Commissioner.

Our mom's legacy includes leading her family out of poverty, confronting her bi-polar mental health illness, placing an emphasis on education, helping those who cannot help themselves and always having high expectations. Mom, on behalf of all of us, especially your children and grandchildren, thank you very much for taking a difficult situation and allowing us opportunities to make a better life. I am proud to say, we are family!

> Life is good!
> Live, Love, and be Grateful!

Although my mom was an important person in my life, my wife became the most important person to me when we were married in 1989. Simply stated, I am an overachiever in the marriage department. We recently celebrated our 35th wedding anniversary. Pastor Frank, from Ft. Wayne, led our wedding ceremony. Included in his message was the statement, "I hope you have 50 years of marriage." We thought the goal was a lifetime together. Jokingly we said, "only 15 more to go."

My wife's maiden name was Jody Beerman. In high school (Heritage HS in Ft. Wayne, Indiana) and in college (Central Michigan University) Jody was a hall of fame basketball player. In high school, she led her team to a state championship and she was named the Indiana Miss Basketball. Then, in college at Central Michigan University, she was a first team academic All-American. To top off her list of achievements, she was voted to have her picture on the Wheaties box. The award was earned when she was in high school. The entire community showed up to eat Wheaties one morning. As it turned out they ate a lot of Wheaties. After other factors were considered, Jody was selected as one of six finalists from across the United States.

However, the NCAA said she could not have her picture on the cereal box until she finished college. When she finally had her picture on the box, and the box was on the store shelves, General Mills sent us hundreds of boxes of Wheaties—which we handed out at our wedding reception.

Jody is described as being incredibly successful in academics and basketball, yet remains very humble. In addition, she is a great mom and a tireless worker at school and home.

One final story involving one of our kids and the Wheaties box. Earlier, I mentioned that we ate our pet goat and I mentioned that our mom would not admit to it for at least a few years later. But give her credit, she finally told us what had happened. Now, part II of the story. Reid, our middle son, had just finished a Little League baseball all-star game, and we all were going to the Dairy Queen for some ice cream treats. When we arrived, we were greeted by one of his all-star teammates and the teammate's two sisters. The girls were wearing dresses—keeping in mind, they were at a baseball game. So, that should have been a clue to not tell the goat story to this family that we had just met. But Reid had other thoughts. So, he tells the story about my siblings and I eating the pet goat. He was expecting the girls to laugh. Instead, their jaws hit the floor and their eyes bugged out. So, Reid in an attempt to try to impress them, immediately said, "but my mom was on the Wheaties box."

After getting married, more than anything, Jody and I wanted a family. So, we had three sons and from the moment they were born, we loved them unconditionally with our whole heart. Ty is the oldest. He graduated from Ferris State University with a four-year degree in Technology. He is employed by a Grand Rapids based technology company. While in high school, Ty was a member of the band. He is smart, hardworking, has a giant heart, is very kind, and loves his brothers and his dog. Reid is the middle child. He graduated from Grand Valley State University, where he earned his degree in finance and played on the baseball team. While in high school, in addition to baseball, Reid also played on the varsity basketball team. He currently works in the finance department at General Motors. He is a lot of fun to be around, and he is highly competitive. Bryce is the youngest son. He graduated from Michigan State University with a degree in Supply Chain Management and a Master's Degree in Finance. He excelled on the MSU baseball team earning many honors and awards including Freshmen All-American Team, MSU stolen base record holder for season and career. He is an all-around great guy. Also, he is highly competitive.

Two additional family members are our daughters-in-law. Bryce married Rachel Baker in 2021 and Reid married Aubri Barsaleau, also in 2021. Aubri and Rachel have added a fresh perspective on life and we love them dearly. Jody is so happy to have some girls in the family.

This is a poem I included in the speech I gave at Bryce and Rachel's wedding reception I gave a similar speech at Reid and Aubri's reception. (Aubri and Rachel have 100% approval ratings from all family and friends).

The Walk-Off Homerun

Bryce and Rachel, you are married now,
congratulations to the both of you.
There is no turning back now the ring is on
the finger you both said I do.
Bryce, what advice can I give you, besides put
the toilet seat down after you are done
A second bit of advice is to keep each other
laughing and keep having lots of fun

As I look at you today, I can't help but get
excited about your future with each other
I hope that you get to experience the many
joyful challenges of being a father and a
mother
Every child is different, one might be athletic
and creative, another funny and clever
When the time comes for a baby sitter think
of the Kelley's first and the Baker's whenever

The years 2020 and 2021 were very
challenging to us and to many of you
The acts of hatred, election craziness, and the
pandemic, just to name a few
As horrific as these things were, Rachel and
Bryce's love continues to grow
Keeping God and family at the center of all
decisions is something that they know

In conclusion,
Rachel, as the father of the groom I must say,
you are getting a great guy in Bryce
I would describe him as being hard working,
smart, loyal, gentle and nice
Bryce you are lucky, as you have married
Rockford's finest, on our list she is #1
Describing Rachel with a baseball term she is
not just a hit, she is a walk-off homerun

GO GREEN! GO WHITE!

I was the fifth of six kids. I have three brothers and two sisters. Pat was the first born. Pat was a tremendous athlete and he lived with our dad in Grand Rapids. He had the state record in throwing the discus. He had an incredible combination of strength and speed—he could bench press more than

400 pounds and ran the 40-yard dash in 4.6 seconds. A serious shoulder injury ended his football career. Kathleen was the next oldest. She was always very kind and she demonstrated persistence by returning to college and earning her bachelor's degree in social work. She lives in Munising, Michigan, and she was an outstanding softball player, too. Michael was the third child. He is always the last one to leave the dinner table. He was a focused athlete, excelling in wrestling and football. Away from sports, he is very calm and quiet. He is a podiatrist in our home town of Rockford, Michigan. Sean is the fourth child. He is the most outgoing in the family. He is a highly respected structural engineer, who went back to college to earn a Master's degree in business. He was a wrestling state champion and he lives in Detroit. Also, he loves traveling around the world. I am the fifth child. I enjoyed playing all sports and had many scholarship offers in baseball and football. My career choice was teaching biology and math. Then moved on to school administration, where I served in a few different positions including high school principal and assistant superintendent of curriculum. Lucia is the youngest, and might be worthy of the most outgoing, sorry Sean. Lucia is an outstanding truck driver and a friend to many. She is very funny, very strong and a pretty good softball player.

A topic of conversation around our house was how I decided to go to CMU. The options came down to the following:

- Northern Michigan University to play football—full ride scholarship

- Michigan Tech University to play football—full ride scholarship

- A number of smaller schools to play baseball—partial scholarships

- Central Michigan University to play baseball—grants, academic scholarships, but no guaranteed baseball money

- Other important information that I had to think about included:

- I was the youngest student in my senior class (not done growing)

- The summer before my senior year, I demonstrated some skills and talent for baseball. Scouts from Cincinnati Reds, Los Angeles Dodgers, and Detroit Tigers came to watch me play. Also, I had a great showing at the Cincinnati Reds tryout. While pitching to a catcher, I was clocked at 83 mph. During the scrimmage, with live hitting/pitching I touched 87 mph. Not bad for a 16-year-old.

- Another player attending the Cincinnati Reds tryout was Kevin Tapani. Kevin was an outstanding pitcher who went on to win 150 games in the major leagues and earned a World Series Championship ring. However, at the Reds tryout I performed better than Kevin.

While I hit 86-87 mph on the radar gun in the afternoon scrimmage, Kevin was at 81 mph (he might have pitched the day before.) I include this information because if I had chosen football, and Kevin went on and won a world championship, I would have thought I could have done the same.

- I had a great senior year in football—1st team all-state.

- The summer after my senior year I had some arm issues and my velocity dropped down to 80-81 mph. At this point I may have reconsidered NMU, but it's so late in the recruiting process that I'm sure they did not have a full-ride scholarship left.

- I decided to attend CMU—no regrets as I have a great job, great friends, and a great wife,

- If I would have made a decision based on sports alone—I would have chosen NMU.

It's important to mention that because of our low family income, we automatically qualified for financial aid. There were many types of financial aid. Some of those included loans, scholarships, and grants. A common component in our financial aid packages was a Pell Grant, which we did not have to pay back.

Another category of interest is "the games kids play." While today's youth are being entertained with 3-D graphics, we were playing games with the neighbor kids like, "who could hold their breath the longest while sitting in a trash barrel." Another U.P. game was "climbing the fuel tower, then jumping off." This is a game that I would not participate. The fuel tower was about 20 feet high and had metal steps that could be used to climb up the side, then jump off and land in a pile of snow. The next person had to go one step higher. This continued until they reached the top, or quit.

Over the years, we have shared many sibling stories. Here is a brief description of a few of these stories. Topping my list of favorite stories include the following; Lucia learning how to count syllables with step dad Larry. Michael's miraculous recovery—so he became a doctor. The horse in Larry's pickup truck. Finally, Kathleen goes shopping at K-Mart with mom.

Lucia is the youngest of the siblings. The first story about her is how she learned to count syllables. She learned of such things as syllables from our step-dad Larry Gould. Larry was "outdoor smart," but struggled with "book smart" things. While he was working with Lucia, he was frequently heard saying, "I can't believe you can't get it through your thick skull, Munising, "Mu" "ni" "si" "n" "g" that's five syllables. Hell, you can't even get the easy ones, like Whale "wh" "ale."—that's two syllables." Lucia did not allow this obstacle to get in her way, as she is an avid reader today.

Another unforgettable experience was when my brother Michael and I went berry picking. Mom always made us berry pick with a safety partner. So, me being the youngest, always got ditched. Well, this time I got ditched again, so I returned to our house. It was getting late and Michael had not returned, yet. As it got darker outside, we were all getting worried. Mom went to a neighbor's house to use their phone. When the Michigan State Police officers arrived, it was nearly midnight. I climbed into the state police car and drove to all of the possible places where Michael might be. Mom was also in the car and about an hour into the search, mom heard a noise. Earlier in the day, Michael reached a few dangling berries on a pile of logs. He lost his balance and before he could get out of the way a 300-pound log rolled on top of him. He could not move. He was under that log for 13 hours, and when the ambulance took him away, he was fighting for his life. This near tragic event had a huge impact on Michael. He always enjoyed helping people, and now he knew that he wanted to help people through the medical profession. He went on to earn his doctorate degree in Podiatric Medicine.

Another story that will always get a chuckle out of me, involved a horse and Larry's truck. My hometown of Shingleton, Michigan has a gas station, a restaurant, and a small grocery store. If you are passing through Shingleton, don't blink, you might miss it. Well on this day, the townies were out in big numbers, maybe twenty-five people. Ten of the men, including step-dad, Larry were hanging out at the gas station. One of the men shouts out "who is that crazy bit—driving a truck with a horse in the back?" Another one of the guys shouts out, "Hey, Larry it looks like your truck. It is your truck and it has a horse in the back." Larry said, "What the hell is she thinking. We can't afford to feed the kids, how can we feed a f---ing horse?"

Mom had another surprise for Larry. She read an article in the Mother Earth magazine. The article was focused on building a six-sided house. To me that seemed a little beyond Larry's skill level. Mom took money from the bank loan and went out and bought six large poles—for thousands of dollars. I think the wooden poles are still rotting in the woods.

After a couple of years, without any progress being made on the hexagonal house, mom canceled the house building and they decided to buy a new trailer. We were all very happy to get running water, shower, bath and sink.

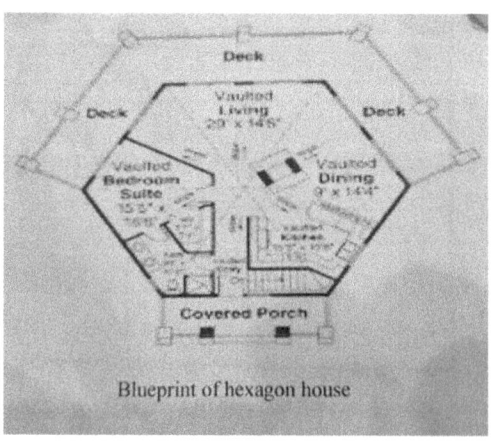

Blueprint of hexagon house

Our Home

Looking back on these times of buying horses and building hexagonal houses, our family members believe these were the signs of mom's mental illness (bi-polar) worsening. As I mentioned earlier, another obvious sign was her showing up unannounced in the middle of the night at our front door, 350 miles away from her home. Mom was first diagnosed with bi-polar disorder. She would seem fairly normal for a while, then she would stop taking her medication and she would return to hospitalization. Another example of bizarre behavior from my mom was an announcement that she was voting for Donald Trump. She was a vocal anti-Trump, anti-Republican her entire life. As a matter of fact, her strong and passionate feelings towards the

Women's Rights Movement was the primary reason for their divorce. We supported mom, through her struggles. We are family!

One final sibling story. Kathleen did not want to go clothes shopping on this particular day. However, our mom wanted to go shopping, but knew she wasn't quite feeling right. So, she told Kathleen that she needed to go with her, just in case our mom had an emergency. Well, at K-Mart, they had a Blue Light Special Sale in aisle 17. My mom actually started running in the store. She was the first shopper to get the scarf and hat combination. However, there was a terrible odor coming from my mom. As it turns out, my mom crapped her pants. She quickly grabbed a welcome mat that was on display and wrapped it around her waist and walked out of the store. When they got to the car, she told Kathleen, "If you had six kids, you would crap your pants, too!"

In summary, I love my brothers and sisters. They are a smart, fun, and a hardworking group. They were good role models. However, over the years it has been fun getting even with them for beating me in so many contests when I was younger. Another interesting fact is that my brother Michael met his future wife, Amy, at our wedding. Also, she was a teammate of Jody's at Central Michigan University.

Parkinson's Disease—the basics

I have been battling Parkinson's Disease for nearly twenty-five years. There are good days and bad days. Inspired by Michael J. Fox, I am actively leading some of the PD (Parkinson's Disease) awareness at the local level. I volunteer with Corewell Health, giving speeches and presentations, in an attempt to help people in a time of need. As you may have predicted, Michael J Fox is one of my heroes. He is the perfect example of the 10-90% Rule.

Getting ready for deep brain stimulation surgery

"Ten percent of your life is determined by what happens to you and ninety percent is determined by how you respond to what happens to you."

In my role as Parkinson's Ambassador, when I first meet with newly diagnosed Parkinson's patients, they feel like their life is over. I explain to them that their lives will change, but their life is not over. With the development and implementation of an appropriate plan, PD patients can live for decades. In the planning process, decisions related to medication, exercise, diet, and maintaining a positive attitude, must be made. Parkinson's patients can live a high quality of life for many, many years. I share my feelings that I believe I am a better person today, because of my Parkinson's experience. I am humbler, caring, accepting and forgiving. I try to enjoy every day by staying positive and maintaining a "live, love, and be grateful" attitude. I still enjoy golfing and having fun with friends. After being diagnosed, I worked another 20+ years for Rockford Public Schools.

I believe that Michael J. Fox's passion, drive, commitment, and leadership will eventually lead to a cure for Parkinson's Disease. It's amazing what a difference one person can make!

My Parkinson's symptoms started when I was 34 years old—24 years ago. It took the doctors two and a half years to accurately diagnose my illness. At the time, I was in the middle of some exciting events in my life. I had just been named the principal of Rockford High School, one of the largest and most respected high schools in Michigan, and my wife and I were expecting the birth of our third child—our son Bryce.

At the time I did not know much about Parkinson's Disease, but I knew that if I wanted to see our three sons graduate from college and get married someday, I would have to learn more about this disease.

I have been retired for six years. Today I am excited to be serving in the role of Parkinson's Ambassador, which is a volunteer position with Corewell Health. I enjoy helping people who have recently been diagnosed with Parkinson's and those who have had it for many years and are considering surgery. My primary message is this, TO BEAT PARKINSON'S DISEASE YOU MUST HAVE A POSITIVE ATTITUDE AND A HEALTHY PERSPECTIVE ON LIFE. Take, for example, my Parkinson's experience. One day I woke up and felt different and it did not go away. Later I was diagnosed with Parkinson's. After a significant amount of reflection, I knew how I needed to respond. I needed to maintain my positive attitude. I needed to have purpose. I needed to increase my weekly amount of exercise. Finally, I needed to be an active member of my care team.

The following quote from Morgan Richard Olivier, helps me keep things in perspective and keeps me positive:

"THEN ONE DAY IT CLICKS.
The pain you had turns into peace as
You accept that everything had to
Happen exactly as it did for you

Exactly who you are now
You hold no blame, bitterness, or
Resentment toward the experience,
Person, or yourself.
Instead, you see it as a catalyst
That led to your change
And development.

The very storm that shook so
Much in you also worked
To clear your path."

If you are battling Parkinson's, it's also important to keep your sense of humor. Comedian Jeff Foxworthy had a skit called "you might be a redneck if." For example, if you cut your grass and find a car, you might be a redneck. Well, I created my own skit, titled, "You might have Parkinson's Disease if…" Here are two examples:

First example, fit bit watch: Last year for Father's Day, my kids got me a fit bit watch. Their goal was to get me in better shape by monitoring how many steps I take every day. So, I go to bed and forget to take it off my wrist. I wake up the next morning and notice that I have nearly 10,000 steps in (must have been an active night). So, if you wake up to your kids wanting to take a walk with you and you tell them, "No thanks, I already have my 10,000 steps in for today," you might have Parkinson's Disease.

The second example, memory test: One of the seven areas that I had to be evaluated in to be eligible for the deep brain stimulation surgery was the "cognitive skills test." After the test, the doctor said, "You have tremendous skills, you have cognitive skills in reserve. My wife jumps into the conversation and says, "is memory included in the testing. The doctor says, "yes, it is." My wife adds another question—"So, if I send my husband to the store for a loaf of bread and a gallon of milk and he comes home with a bag of potato chips and some Mountain Dew, should I accept that?" The doctor said "heavens no, he is very capable."

So, if you think you can manipulate the evaluation system to get your doctor to tell your wife that you can have unlimited pop and chips, you might have Parkinson's Disease.

Deep brain stimulation – DBS Surgery

People with Parkinson's Disease need to continue to live active lives. Daily exercise must be taking place. A catch phrase to emphasize the importance of this is "running water does not freeze." Keep running, Keep moving, Keep fighting.

Most PD patients come to a point when the medicine loses its effectiveness. At that time, the discussion turns to surgery options. Deep brain stimulation (DBS) surgery is a common choice for patients that need relief from their primary symptoms. Following surgery, the doctors usually see significant improvement in the patient's dyskinesia, tremors, slowness, reduction in the dosage of medicine, etc.

The DBS surgery includes drilling holes in the skull and implanting wire leads to specific parts of the brain. These electrodes are connected to a pulse generator/pacemaker, which is then implanted under the skin in the chest wall. A computer controls the pulse generator, which sends electrical signals to the brain."

One of my enjoyments in life is writing and reading poetry. Here is an example:

Ten Million and One

Hello, my name is Ryan I'm 58 years old and have Parkinson's Disease
I have had this disease for 24 years, can you give me a hand and help, please
Parkinson's is a progressive movement disorder that has no known cure
Ten million people have Parkinson's, it's a high number that's for sure

When I talk to other Parkinson's patients, I tell them life is still great
Keep living your best life for as long as you

can, don't sit and wait
One of the keys is to exercise—walk, jog, lift
weights, and stretch
Get creative and think of ways to keep
moving, play with a dog—FETCH!

A goal for each of us is to try and help others
and to live our best life,
I have developed a care team, consisting of my
doctor, my sons and my wife
Everyone in the process should be excited with
all of the research being done
Hopefully, very soon we can sound the
trumpets, victory will have been won

We all should give thanks to Michael J Fox,
Kirk Gibson, and Muhammad Ali
Some locally who deserve praise are Dr.
Sririm, Kelly McWilliams and Angie
We all must give it everything we've got, to get
this disease over and done
We do not want our grandpa, dad, or son to
become number ten million and one

THE G.O. A.T.
(The Greatest Grandma Of All Time)

Jody's mom, Doris Beerman, is everyone's favorite grandparent. Kids are drawn to her like a magnet. In her honor, we wrote her this poem.

It was great that we got to exercise our right to vote last week on election day
However, I wish we could have had a new category "best grandma," What do you say?
Grandma Beerman would have been a runaway winner, because she is our hero
When I last checked on grandma she had a lead in the polls, 100% to zero

As many of you know Grandma "rules the roost," she is "chief in charge"
She will help anybody with a problem, she will solve it, small or large
She is the leader of her family, and she shows love every second of every day
She knows how to raise a family she should write a book titled "The Beerman Way"

The Beerman Way is a recipe for success, happiness, and love
It combines hard work, honesty, and when you don't have the answer, look above

One thing is for certain. If you need 25 cents, here's 3 nickels and a dime
She is a lock for the title of The Greatest Grandma Of All Time

———————————

Life Lesson 1: Things don't always work out the way you planned it, but life can still be filled with purpose and fun.

Life Lesson 2: Parkinson's Disease has changed my life, but it has not ended my life. I look forward to many more "best life days".

Photos

Sometimes it's nice to put a face with a name. You have read about each of the people in my family, now here are the pictures that go along with each of the names and each of the stories.

Humble Beginnings (left to right): Lucia Gedrey, Ryan Kelley, Kathleen Kelley, Michael Kelley, Sean Kelley

The Beerman Family: (left to right)
Marcia Beerman, Brad Beeman, Larry Beerman
Jody Kelley, Doris Beerman, Ryan Kelley, Vicki Roop

Little League Baseball—glad nobody can see my boots

Chapter 2—My Extended Family

*I was hoping that I would never have to
tell you this, but "yes, we ate our
pet goat Paint."*

As you are aware, in most situations it takes an entire group of individuals to accept their defined roles, for the team to be successful. Teachers, parents, students, secretaries, custodians, and many others must collaborate to develop a success plan for every student. The same is true in the medical profession. Patients must have an active care team to give them the best opportunity to live their highest quality of life. Another example is a family. Each member has expectations that must be met. Included in this group are "extended family members". These vary from family to family.

For my entire life I have been surrounded by students and educators. That is why I consider many to be extended family members. I began my career teaching math and science at the age of twenty-two. Then, I moved into administration, where I served in the roles of middle school assistant principal at age twenty-six, high school assistant principal at twenty-eight, middle school principal at thirty, high school principal at thirty-four, and assistant superintendent at forty-two.

K-12 education is challenging for everyone. I believe there are many reasons for this, including I think the breakdown of the family unit has resulted in schools being required to do the work that used to belong to the parents. If teachers are required to take on these duties, they must be provided training and support—for example, when working with challenging topics such as transgenders, school safety, social media, and mental health. These are all serious topics that require professional development. In addition to reading and learning on my own, I did get assistance from my mentors, including our pastors. I believe it is important to understand multiple perspectives before passing judgment. Also, despite the many benefits of technology, we are aware of the many risks that exist, including artificial intelligence.

Here are a few examples of some interesting student situations that took place over the past 31 years at Rockford Public Schools. How can you not laugh or cry at these daily occurrences?

Nickname

Rusty, a special needs student, walked up to me in the hallway and said, "Hi Mr. Kelley, do you know that I have a nickname? I said, Rusty, you're a good man and it does not surprise me that you have a nickname." Rusty said, "I know I am a good man; do you want to guess what my nickname is? I said, "with a name like Rusty it's probably something like Rusty nail or Rusty bench." Rusty said "nice try, but you're not even close. It's Paul."

Parent teacher conferences

During parent teacher conferences, a parent sat down with the physical education teacher and said, "I'm surprised my son received a "D" in your class. Immediately the teacher apologized and began to explain why the "D" was appropriately assigned. The parent quickly interrupted him and said, "No apology is necessary, I want to thank you for the "D." My son and I had a deal that if he could get "C's" in every class, he would earn $100. It's been a rough month and we don't have the $100!"

Snow day

The morning of a bad weather snow day, a very upset individual drove to the middle school saying that he was shocked that the school bus still had not picked up his children. He said that his wife told him that they have been waiting for 30 minutes. When I explained that there was no school because of the snow day, he asked who he needed to call to have their school closings appear on the Disney Channel because their family does not watch the local news.

The mule

A student at the high school was kicked off the bus for two days. The very next day his father showed up at school with a mule at the front door and said this is what you will be riding home if you get kicked off the bus again. The mule then did a number two on the sidewalk. Not missing a beat, the dad said, "That reminds me, your mom is tired of your crap, too!"

Happy birthday

One day during lunch duty, a very shy special needs student told me it was her birthday. A football player overheard this, and with about 20 of his teammates, all wearing their jerseys, sang Happy Birthday to her. Afterwards, with tears in her eyes, she said that was the nicest thing that anyone has done for her.

Mickey Mouse

A new student came to us in the middle of the school year and I knew she had a troubled past, but I was unclear as to what the issues were, but I was about to find out. On this day, a teacher brought the girl to the office and said she was very rude in class. When she got to my office, I told the student my name was Dr. Kelley, the principal, and student behavior was very important to me. Her response was "Well whooped-tee-doo, aren't you special. What do you want, a medal, a chocolate chip cookie, or a Mickey Mouse pen?" I began to walk out of my office to go read her student file. I then turned around and said, "I think I will take the Mickey Mouse pen"—which I thought was a cute response. Then, she immediately came back with, "Why don't you take your happy ass down to the store and buy one?"

Some things are more important than math

Two days before Christmas break, a student with tears in his eyes, told his math teacher that he had to leave the classroom. When asked why, the student did not answer, and just left the room. When he arrived in my office, I had to ask him what was bothering him. After a few minutes, he explained that a few weeks prior his father had kicked him out of his house, as well as his mother. Furthermore, the only place they have been staying at was at his girlfriend's house. On that particular day, prior to going to math class, his girlfriend had broken up with him. (I have to add that our counselors, teachers, and administrators all worked together to help this family through a difficult time.)

Milk, it builds a body good

David, a special needs student, and his mom would call me every night at 11:00 PM. On this night she called to say that David was very excited to tell me that he got hit by a car, while riding his bike. The next morning David was running down the hallway to tell me about his accident. He said that his head put a dent in the people's car, as well as shattering the windshield. I said "David, you are lucky, are you okay? He said, yup—you know I drink a lot of milk."

He doesn't treat her like a mom…

A father asked to meet with me because his son had just been assigned a suspension for harassing a female student. After explaining what had happened, the father responded, "I don't know why my son doesn't respect women. He doesn't even respect his mom. He never listens to her; he swears at her. He doesn't treat her like a mom, he treats her like a wife!"

The light is on, but nobody is home

One morning a teacher caught a girl smoking in the boys' bathroom and sent her to the office to see me. When I asked the girl why she would do such a thing, she said... "because the lights were out in the girls' bathroom."

Special Olympics

Our special education students are a joy to work with. I remember a special moment that took place at the Special Olympics Games. I had just walked into the gym and I saw Kyle hustling after a ball that went out of bounds. However, Kyle saw me walking in and he ran across two other basketball courts and gave me a big hug. After thanking him, I told him to hustle back to his game. He said that he would, but he needed to finish his hug first.

Whatever it takes

The mother of a high school student stopped into my office to make me aware of a situation. She said that there was a conspiracy against her son. She said that her son was a gifted athlete, but the middle school and high school coaches cut him during tryouts in basketball and baseball. Then, the conversation got weird. She told me to sit back and relax because she was going to give me lap dance, so long as her son was placed on a team. I explained that this is not a part of the tryout process.

———————————

And we liked it!

Growing up in the 1970's in the U.P., we did not have any fun, electronic games to play with. Here is a brief description of three of the games we did play.

- Trash can game

  Each "contestant" took a turn in the trash can, holding his/her breathe for as long as possible. My brothers would always "take care of me" by having me go last. The goal was to hold your breath for as long as possible. Nearly every game ended with me out of breath and my brothers not letting me out of the trash can.

- Fuel tank jump

  Along with our house on Mill Street in Shingleton, was a 20-foot-high fuel tank that had metal steps projecting out from the side of the tower. The game was simple—when it was your turn to jump, you climbed one step higher than the person before you, and jumped down into s pile of snow, remembering to create a new pile of snow on the ground. I am proud to say I never won this game.

- Apple baseball

  To play regular baseball, you need bats, gloves, balls, etc. Not having any money, we played apple baseball. Apple baseball does not require balls, gloves or bats. We substituted apples for baseballs, hands for gloves, and a small branch for the bat. Instead of the pitcher throwing the apple to the catcher, the pitcher handed the apple to the batter. The batter would attach the apple to the branch by poking a hole through the center of the apple, and swing the branch as hard as he could. Any apple that went past the railroad tracks was a homerun!

———————

Load up the truck

During the hot summer days, it was common to pile into the truck and go to Clear Lake. It was only a ten-minute drive and we would bring along a football, a frisbee, and a bar of Fels Naptha soap to take a bath. It was a simple activity, but we really looked forward to it.

Merry Christmas in the U.P.

The holidays for our family were not as bad as you might expect. When you don't have any money, you don't have high expectations for gifts. A typical Christmas gift giving was mom getting each of us an individual present and we would all share a family gift. Examples of individual gifts included, belts, hats, socks and underwear. The family gift was usually practical and something that we needed. Examples of this include a used chain saw, used refrigerator, and outdated *World Book Encyclopedia.*

Additionally, we would get a nice present from Joe
and Marie Gould, Larry's parents

We had a nice dinner each Christmas.

Faith

I gave a speech to a Parkinson's Disease
support group in 2021. After everyone left, an older
gentleman approached me and said, "You forgot
to mention one of the most powerful ways to beat
Parkinson's. Through the power of prayer." Jody
and I want to live our lives closer to Jesus. And
we want the rest of our family to join us in heaven
someday. Leading us in our journey, have been some
outstanding pastors. For me, there are two that stand
out. Pastor Bickel at Immanuel Lutheran in Grand
Rapids, Michigan and Pastor Love at St. Peters
Lutheran. Both are members of our extended family.

Pastor Love led our sons through the
confirmation process. We felt very fortunate to be
members at the church with him as the pastor. When
he received a Call to consider becoming the pastor
of a larger church in Toledo, I had to let him know
what he meant to me and to our family. However, at
the last minute, I decided to wait and give the letter
to him after he had made his decision. So, I wrote the
following letter, and gave it to him (To clarify, Pastor
Love turned down the original Call to the church in
Toledo. However, three years later, he accepted the

Call in Toledo.) We were all very sad to see him go, but we also felt thankful that we had an extra three years of his leadership.

Dear Pastor Love,

The primary purpose of this letter is to tell you how happy/relieved we are that you decided to stay at St. Peters. Your impact on our family and our congregation has been overwhelming.

Prior to you reaching your decision, I started to write a letter, trying to let you know how much we hoped that you would stay in Rockford. However, it gave me a feeling of selfishness because I wrote it from a "what's best for me" perspective. So, rather than writing a letter, I prayed for you that you would do what was best for you and your family, and go where you could do the greater good.

I'm sure that there are aspects of your job that I am unaware, but from everything that I have witnessed, I am continually left with the feeling that "we are so fortunate to have Pastor Love as the leader of our church." Your sermons are powerful, with messages that connect to every member of the congregation. Your passion is evident whenever you speak. In terms of leadership, a person's effectiveness is determined in the tough times—I can't imagine a more confusing time for people than David Kohl's battle with leukemia. I left the funeral service with a sense of peace and comfort for David's family and friends. Additionally, I left the service with a strong sense of pride that I attend a church led by Pastor Love—I was glad that those in attendance were able to hear the message that I get to hear every Sunday.

I always hope for the best, but prepare for the worst. Last Sunday, I was prepared for your decision to leave St. Peters. I had planned on telling you that the only way I could approach this was to handle it in a similar manner as to when I attend a funeral—"I could mourn your leaving, or celebrate the three years we learned from you." Fortunately, my hopes came true and we can celebrate your extended stay. You have been a blessing to all of us!

I can only imagine what you have experienced the past few weeks—I'm sure that you are emotionally fatigued. Please take a break and use the enclosed gift card to take Diane out to dinner at Reds. Thanks for all that you do!

Obstacles

We are all going to face obstacles in our lives. Some of these obstacles may be serious in nature. There may be other situations that are less life changing. Examples of obstacles are, health related, financial matters, and family matters. The best advice that I can give is to never give up when facing obstacles. You might need help to overcome certain obstacles. You may need to lean on somebody! Don't be afraid to ask/pray for assistance. Keep a positive attitude.

Many students in our public schools are faced with financial obstacles. They may want to be involved in after-school activities, such as music, drama, and athletics, however, they cannot afford fees for equipment or uniforms. Furthermore, these students are unable to find transportation home after practice and games because their parents do not have a working vehicle. My brothers and I were faced with this obstacle many times. Whenever a ride was not available, as a last resort, we would try hitch-hiking.

Hitchhiking was easy, but it was also potentially dangerous. Depending upon who was in the other car, you could be lucky or you could become a victim. All you had to do was walk down the road and when you heard a car coming up next to you, stick out one of your thumbs. I remember a van stopping and when they opened the back door, a cloud of green smoke left the van. The driver of the vehicle asked if he could give me a ride. I said, "No thank you sir, I like to walk."

My brothers and I were fortunate to have some nice friends and neighbors, especially the Jim and Deanna Blank family. They gave us rides home after many practices and games.

Laughter

One of our high school English teachers, Mr. C., told me that one of his students was having a rough day. After repeated interruptions from the student, Mr. C. finally shouted out "If you don't shut up, I'm going to drop you like a dime in a phone booth!" The student response was "Ok, but what is a phone booth?

Mentors

I have had the good fortune of working with some outstanding people. I have learned many good and helpful things from my mentors. The two mentors that I need to recognize are Jim Landfair and Jamie Hosford. Jim was a middle school teacher and administrator, who took a personal interest in me. Most of our discussion took place on the golf course. Most of my discussion with Jamie took place in his office, with some carry-over onto the golf course. Jim and Jamie were awesome people who lit up every room they entered. Jamie would provide advice in many areas, included the following:

1. Celebrate the good things

2. Family comes first

3. Do the right thing

4. Good conquers evil

5. Laugh at yourself frequently

6. It is what it is!

Jim Landfair—mentor

Jamie Hosford—mentor

I feel very fortunate that Jim and Jamie saw something in me that was worth their time and attention. Not a day goes by when I don't think of them.

My extended family: teachers

I think that every one of our outstanding teachers is underpaid. They work many hours outside of the school day and many times use money out of their own pockets to purchase student learning activities. They are dedicated and committed to improving the quality of life for their students.

Reflecting upon my 30+ years working at Rockford Public Schools, I have many wonderful memories. I really enjoyed working in a collaborative environment. Every year there were hundreds of educators who helped students accomplish great things. One of the high school teachers who stopped into my office on a regular basis was Jerry Thompson. On this, the last day of his 37-year teaching career, Jerry stopped in to see me. He handed me a piece of paper that had a list of items on it. The list was titled, "The most important things I learned while working with high school students throughout my career." Here is his list:

- Smile
- Catch them doing something right
- Keep high academic standards and model them
- Model behaviors they will need, even if you don't have them
- Remember they see you when you don't see them
- Keep your energy level high
- Don't use negative sarcasm
- Be consistent
- Return their work and tests fast; develop techniques to do so, i.e. staggered test days and essays
- Smile more
- Defend the profession with pride and dignity

Another highly respected Rockford High School teacher is Mr. Fred Reusch. I asked him what were some of the reasons for his students' success. Listed below are some of his abbreviated responses:

- Develop a solid understanding of the content you are teaching. Never go into a class unprepared.
- Improve every year.
- If you make a mistake, don't try to cover it up.
- Challenge students—have high expectations.
- Build relationships with students. Attend their after-school activities.
- Be fair at all times.

Many of the items on the above list can be used to help teachers build relationships with students and other staff members. The following statement has been adopted by our teachers, "Students don't care how much you know, until they know how much you care!" This is true whether you are from Munising, Michigan, Rockford, Michigan, Djibouti, or anywhere there are schools. Teachers like Jerry Thompson and Fred Reusch are special. These are the teachers that need to be identified to serve in the role of mentor-teacher.

Newly hired teachers are eager to learn from their mentors. Using myself as an example, during my first hour of my first day of student-teaching at Grandville High School in Grandville, Michigan I had what I thought was a well-designed lesson plan.

To save time for the students I wrote the notes on the board and had distributed a worksheet ahead of time. I tried to maximize instruction time. It did not play out like I had planned. I started the lesson at 7:50 AM and was done at 8:03 AM. My 45-minute lesson plan was done in 13 minutes. Wow, I had a lot to learn. Here I was standing in front of 32 students, wondering what to do next. I decided to learn more about my students by asking questions about their past, present and future. Afterwards, my supervising teacher asked what I would have done differently, if I could teach the lesson again. I told him I would have started the lesson by asking the students questions— it's never too early to build that relationship.

Thinking of the education that I received back at Munising High School in Munising, Michigan, I feel fortunate. I think of some of my favorite teachers. Mrs. Helen Peters and Mr. Jim Landfair were outstanding educators that approached teaching as a calling. Students were attracted to them because they could feel their teachers' caring and kindness. The students always knew that Mr. Landfair and Mrs. Peters were in their corner, wanting them to be successful. In addition to their classroom teaching, they were leaders in after-school activities—Mrs. Peters in theater and Mr. Landfair in athletics. They promoted a balanced education.

Mark Twain said, "The two most important days of your life are the day you were born and the day you find out why." For our teachers, the day they began to see how they can change a student's life, they knew why they were born.

Another area of discussion for families is, what are the three or four most important decisions you will make in your lifetime. For many people, the Big Three topic areas are:

1. Choosing your faith

2. Choosing your spouse

3. Choosing your career

I will add a fourth:

4. Choosing your attitude

Many people look at 'attitude' as a personality trait that you are born with. However, I believe that your attitude is something that you choose. It's a conscious choice made by every person, every day.

We are in this together—We Are Family!

My extended family: pets

If you are the owner of a pet, you are well aware that they are important members of today's families. Pets can encourage companionship and nurturing behavior. They also teach us to assist with mental health issues. Many schools have therapy dogs to better meet the students' emotional needs.

Over the years we have had many types of pet dogs at our house—small, medium, large, extra-large, smart, stupid, full of love, forgiving, helpful, and useless. Also, they come in many colors and shapes. In addition to the pet dogs, we also had pet goats, chickens, ducks, horses, and roosters. Many children and adults had best friends that were pets. Some pets are fortunate to receive birthday gifts and parties, food from the refrigerator, baths at the pet spa, and unlimited treats. Our pets were not so fortunate.

However, every one of our pets received love and attention. In return, the pets gave us things to laugh at and things to learn—very similar to our children. Here are some examples:

- Our first dog, may have been our best dog. Caesar was a Great Pyrenees, all white, and weighed about 75 pounds. He was smart, handsome, and very protective of us kids. Whether he was laying on top of us protecting us from the cold weather, or protecting us by barking at strangers, Caesar was in charge.

There was a neighbor man that offered us $100 for Caesar and mom told him that the dog was not for sale. We are family!

- Whitey was a purebred mutt. He weighed seven or eight pounds, soaking wet. He is best remembered for jumping into the hole in the outhouse, landing in a pile of poop. Somehow Sean was involved, so he was in charge of getting Whitey out of the hole and the clean-up that followed.

- Then, there was Bo, the boxer. He was a big stud, with a brindle coat. No dog or person would ever think about messing with us when Bo was present. Some nights he would sleep at the base of Ty's crib. Unfortunately, when Jody would take Ty out of the crib, Bo would lash out at Jody and one time bit her on the shoulder. As painful as that was for Jody, it was equally painful for me to have Bo put to sleep. But we all agreed that we had to take this action.

- Charlie, the wiener dog, was full of love and empty on smarts. Whenever it was time for him to go into his cage he would run to the same corner in the living room, where the tv stand met the wall. He would stick his nose into the corner hoping this would be the one

time that we would not see him. It was so
funny to see this wiener dog having 95% of
his body out in the open and at the same time
thinking that we can't see him.

- Copper was a labradoodle and he had a broken
  back and was in a lot of pain. Once again, the
  veterinarian and our family members agreed
  that Copper should not live in constant pain.
  Then, the vet asked me if I wanted to feed
  Copper his dream meal. The veterinarian came
  back with—eight Hershey chocolate candy
  bars. Copper ate all eight bars in about thirty
  seconds.

- We also had a goat named Paint, a horse
  named Champ, and a chicken named
  Momma Hen.

- Here are the two granddogs:

Luna (Bryce and Rachel)

Mozzie (Reid and Aubri)

Chapter 3—Overcoming Childhood Poverty

But my mom was on the Wheaties Box.

To overcome poverty, you first need to be highly motivated. My motivation came from my experience as a little boy. Going to school with dirty, stinky clothes was embarrassing. I also had to wear leather boots with my little league baseball uniform. On top of that, we had to get the free lunch tickets that were always a different color. Also, not having a working vehicle prevented any chance of making new friends. It also was embarrassing to have any friends over to our house, as it was not very nice. Even though I was very young, I still remember each and every day of my life in poverty.

We never blamed anyone for our situation. We just accepted it and knew that we would never have our kids or grandkids have to experience that embarrassment. It's difficult to gain any kind of confidence under those circumstances.

There are many ways to approach poverty. Most likely you will develop short term and long-term strategies to help you overcome obstacles. Strategies should include the following:

- Make education your top priority
- Read and study every night
- Join a school team or club
- Hang around friends that want you to be a success.
- Start thinking about a career that matches your interests, skills, and salary needs.

Some of my friends took a different approach. Upon graduating from high school, they started full-time employment. Whether it was a special skill they possessed or a local factory job, they wanted to always have money in their pocket, immediately after graduation and beyond. They did not want to wait four years to get a paycheck.

The educators want to give every student the confidence and knowledge to be successful in whatever career path interests them. We all must work together and get the children to believe that their hopes and dreams can come true. Who knows? You might be the next person on the cover of the Wheaties box.

As mentioned earlier, the picture above serves as a visual reminder, of where our family started. In the photo, from left to right are my siblings—I included their employment and education. Lucia (high school diploma and truck driving school certification), Ryan (retired public school administrator, Central Michigan University undergraduate and Eastern Michigan University doctorate degree), Kathleen (Northern Michigan University undergraduate, social worker), Michael (Michigan Tech undergraduate and Dr. Scholl's School of Podiatric Medicine) and Sean (Michigan Tech University structural engineer and business owner). We certainly have made improvements to our status in the community.

At times I have shown the photo (of us holding animals) to friends to see what their reaction is. Usually, they will say something they think is funny but is really hurtful and think nothing of it. In the words of Walt Whitman "Be curious, not judgmental!" If you are curious about something, ask questions. Do not pass judgment until you have the viewpoint of all involved. When looking at the photo, don't assume the worst until you had a chance to ask questions. (This is Life Lesson 6. It will addressed in chapter 6)

At first, my siblings and I experienced teasing growing up in the Upper Peninsula. We had some people try to make themselves feel better, by being cruel to those less fortunate. However, as we got older, we started to make a name for ourselves. I believe that most people wanted to see us succeed and were proud of our achievements.

As we reflect on our childhood, a question that I always struggle answering is "What would we be doing today, if our parents would have stayed together, and did not get a divorce?" My siblings and I are all at different places with this question. Some feel like our mom took the kids up to the U.P. to make our dad upset. Others think she made a huge sacrifice, by leaving her husband and getting out of an unhealthy situation.

After the divorce, we only saw our dad one week every summer. I always looked forward to that week—a chance to be with my dad. I was very proud of him. He was tall, muscular, and larger than life in my eyes. He was a high school teacher and coach. My dad is still alive, but I have not spoken to him about this. Maybe this book will be reason enough to talk about our childhood. I'm sure that he is proud of us, and wishes he could have seen us more often. I'm sure he has some regrets, too.

On the other side of things, our step-dad, Larry Gould, was not a physically impressive man. He was short, with a huge stomach, and a scruffy beard. He was a simple man who never made it past the comic section of the newspaper. We would joke with Larry and asked him if he wanted the Dow Jones section. He always would say that he would embarrass me by threatening to wear old ugly clothes to my sporting event, and shouting, "That's my boy Ryan Kelley." It was like I had another older brother picking on me. Now that I'm a grown up, the comments weren't that big a deal. On the positive side of things, I think Larry had a good heart and provided some financial resources with his job at the lumber mill. Also, I have nice memories of Larry's parents. Playing two penny ante poker with the adults was the best time for a ten-year-old boy who loved playing cards. Thank you!

Photos

Kathleen's Family (left to right): Norah,
Kathleen Heyrman, Sean Kelley, Cassie, Ava

Lucia with many family members,
and Casey and Cristopher

Megan Kelley, Jacob Kelley, Jael Kelley, Michael Kelley, Amy Kelley, Shannon Dickinson, holding James Dickinson, Mitch Dickinson, Joseph and Anna Kelley, Anna holding Adeline Dickinson

Daniel Anya, Sean Kelley, Morgan Anya, Aaron Kelley

Bryce Kelley, Rachel Kelley, Reid Kelley, Aubri Kelley,
Jody Kelley, Ryan Kelley, Ty Kelley

Chapter 4—How to Fight Parkinson's Disease

"Hey, nice (baseball) cleats, are those steel-toed boots?"

I am one of the 10 million people who has Parkinson's Disease. I am fifty-eight years old and I have had PD for twenty-four years. I have been inspired by the involvement and the commitment of many famous people like Michael J. Fox, Kirk Gibson, and Muhammad Ali. As a result of witnessing their commitment, I have become more active in speaking at community functions, support groups, and care team meetings. Everyone has a part in this war on Parkinson's. While our brilliant researchers are trying to find a cure, the rest of us need to be developing plans for our current PD population. Everyone needs to have hope. Hope that they can maintain their best life for as many years as possible. Listed below are the four battles that we must win.

Battle #1—Awareness/Education/Information

All of us need to be aware of the 10 million people effected by PD. Once we are aware of the size of our challenge, we need to promote the purpose of our efforts. What can we do to help the PD community? We need to educate those who have recently been diagnosed with PD. We need to help them get off to a good start with the development of a personalized success plan. Included in this plan will be an exercise component.

Twenty-four years ago, when I was diagnosed, I had a doctor from Yale tell me and my wife to quit our jobs and travel. He could not have said anything worse to my wife, Jody. I am the optimist in our marriage. Jody is the exact opposite. I asked the doctor why he would say such a thing. He said that his mother died from Parkinson's, and he had never seen another illness so bad. The other obvious question that I had was, could he give me a travel loan? After all, we were 35 years old, with three young children and not much in the savings account. (His advice may have been acceptable, had we been in our 80's.)

Battle #2—Inspiration

I can honestly say that I am a better person because of my Parkinson's experience. Now I am humble, forgiving, understanding and caring. I will still be the first in line to receive the cure, but in the meantime, I will try to continue to become a better person. We cannot sit around and wait for a cure. We need to keep moving, keep thinking, and keep fighting. We need to maintain a positive attitude and a proper perspective. As the care teams develop their plans, an underlying goal is to see their loved ones being happy. However, most of us are uncertain of what happiness is and how to obtain it. I'm reminded of the following letter that was written by a frustrated elderly man:

"We convince ourselves that life will be better after we get married and have a couple of babies. Then, we are frustrated that the kids aren't old enough and we will be content when they are. Then, we're frustrated that we have teenagers to deal with. We will certainly be happy after they get out of that stage. We tell ourselves that life will be complete when our spouse gets his or her act together, when we get a nicer car, when we are able to go on a nice vacation or when we retire. The truth is there is no better time to be happy than right now. If not now, when? Your life will always be filled with obstacles, and time waits for nobody."

Battle #3—Personal success plan developed by care team

A significant amount of time and thought must be put into the development of a care team success plan. Here are some components of my plan:

- Medication—Carbidopa/levodopa (2 pills, every 2 hours), Amantadine (1 pill, 3 times daily), and Pramipexole (1 pill daily in the early afternoon)
- Surgeries—DBS (deep brain stimulation) and SCS (spinal cord stimulation)

- Exercise—cardio (treadmill or stationary bike—15-20 mins), weights (dumbbells and free weights—10-15 mins), stretching and balance (10 mins)
- 35—45 mins per session
- 5 days per week
- Weekly total (175—225 mins)
- Reduce the amount of sugar in diet, drink a lot of water, and eat more fruits and vegetables.
- Continue to be active with educating the community on PD.

Battle #4—A cure

We also need to educate those within the PD community. I frequently speak to the newly diagnosed patients. At first, they seem to have given up hope for a better tomorrow. They feel like they received a death sentence. I make it very clear that Parkinson's will change your life, it will not end your life. We still have a lot of work to do, but we are making progress. However, until we have a cure, we need to keep up the fight. Our first line of defense is bringing awareness to the challenges and limitations of PD. Second, we need to maintain a positive attitude and a proper perspective. Third, each patient and their care team must develop and implement a plan for success. We cannot sit around and wait for a cure. We need to keep moving, keep thinking, and keep fighting.

The first "cure" will be achieved when we are able to prevent the disease from progressing any further. The patient will not have the disease advance any further, but will not get back to "as good as new." The second "cure" will be defined as when the patient, regardless of how long they have had Parkinson's, returns to their previous normal self.

How should our "best life" be defined. To me it should include some of the following: people furthering their education, working hard, staying positive, treating people with respect, and being trustworthy. Be the kind of person that brightens up a room when entering, not when leaving. Be an inspiration. Be a person who wants to attack Parkinson's Disease and is willing to fight, fight, fight. Continue to participate in some of your social activities—golf, cards, watching grandkids activities, etc. Have a legacy to be remembered as a person who fought the disease with a positive attitude, a thirst for knowledge, daily exercised his/her mind and body, kept things in the proper perspective, and was always willing to help his fellow Parkinson's friends— whatever their needs might be! Every Parkinson's patient is different, so each of them will have a plan that is specific to their symptoms. Their care team must be involved in the process.

As the care teams develop their plans, an underlying goal is to see their loved ones being happy. However, most of us are uncertain of what happiness is and how to obtain it. Don't let Parkinson's be your only reason for not being happy. It certainly can be a reason for having a bad day, but don't let it be the sole factor that dominates your life.

If there ever was a group of people who deserve some relief in the form of happiness, it's the 10 million people with Parkinson's Disease and the millions of caregivers. The daily challenges that our Parkinson's community faces can be overwhelming. But we can't give up and sit around while we wait for a cure. We each need to continue to work on being the best we can be.

Life Lesson 3: When I received my Parkinson diagnosis at age thirty-five, I prayed that I would still be alive to enjoy my kids' weddings and meet any future grandchildren at that time. At the weddings, our friends and guests, seeing me in a wheelchair, commented that it must be sad not to dance with your wife and daughters-in-law. I responded with: "Actually it is a bit sad but I am so grateful to be able to be present for this celebration with my family. I feel fortunate."

Life Lesson 4: To overcome your obstacles, you must develop a personalized plan for success.

Chapter 5—
Maintaining Hope

*I hope you know that one person can
make a difference.*

As I reflect on how we raised our kids, I'm sure we made mistakes—everyone does. But all-in-all, we encouraged them to make use of their blessings. We could not be more proud of each of them. They are good people and they will be good parents. Here is a list of some the life lessons that we hope the kids have learned.

Our Top 10 lessons learned and words to live by:

10. Every person has purpose

9. Every day is a new day—a fresh start

8. One person can make a difference

7. Give me a place to stand and I can change the world

6. Hard work beats talent every time

5. Spend time with people who make you laugh.

4. Don't let negative people bring you down

3. Forgiveness is powerful

2. 10% of your life is determined by what happens to you. 90% is determined by how you respond to what happens to you.

1. Don't cry because it's over, smile because it happened.

I believe that every family and every individual should reflect on their lives on a regular basis. Get up every morning, asking what you can do to give you purpose and to help others. One thing that everyone can do is pray for the Parkinson's Disease doctors, nurses, and patients (and any other people, working on trying to find a cure for serious illness). Also, read the research that is taking place, that is bringing renewed hope to the Parkinson's Community. Being one of those who has the disease, I plan on continuing to live my life one day at a time. I will dedicate my life to maintain purpose by helping others.

As I reflect on my life, I hope that I was able to live a life that allowed me to help people, to overcome obstacles. I hope that I served a purpose that was aligned with the phrase "It's not where you start that's important, it's where you finish." I want to know that I am still growing and learning. You must live your life with gratitude. Be thankful for everything that you have.

Hope List 2024

I hope that...

- your life is good
- you live, love, and are grateful
- you know there is no substitute for hard work
- you laugh often
- you learn something new every day
- you can maintain purpose in your life
- you show someone who needs a pick-me-up, that you believe in them
- you reflect upon the people who deserve your thanks, and then give it
- you stay positive, especially around your family and friends
- you take the time to thank the people you love the most
- you ask questions, whenever you need help
- you pray daily
- you feel valued by your family
- you know it's not where you start that's important, it's where you finish
- you enjoyed reading my story

Life Lesson 5: One person can change the world.

Chapter 6—Grandkids, Reflection, and Poetry

"If I can offer you one piece of advice, it would be: quit your jobs and travel."

I have been told by many people that being a grand-parent is ten times more enjoyable than being a parent. Part of the reason for this is, as a parent, you still have to be the disciplinarian. Our middle son, Reid, and his wife Aubri, gave us our first grandchild a few days ago. When Owen Jay Kelley was born, Jody and I were supposed to be in Florida on spring vacation. However, we were not going to miss being introduced to Owen, and we were not going to miss Owen being introduced to the world. He was born on Good Friday, March 29, 2024. In a word, he is "perfect."

Life Lesson 6: "Be curious, not judgmental." This quote has been credited to Walt Whitman. It stresses the importance of people to be curious and ask questions to find out the truth. However, to find out the truth, you must ask questions of people on all sides of the situation. Again, reserve judgment until all have had the chance to speak. This is one of the most important life lessons we can teach our kids.

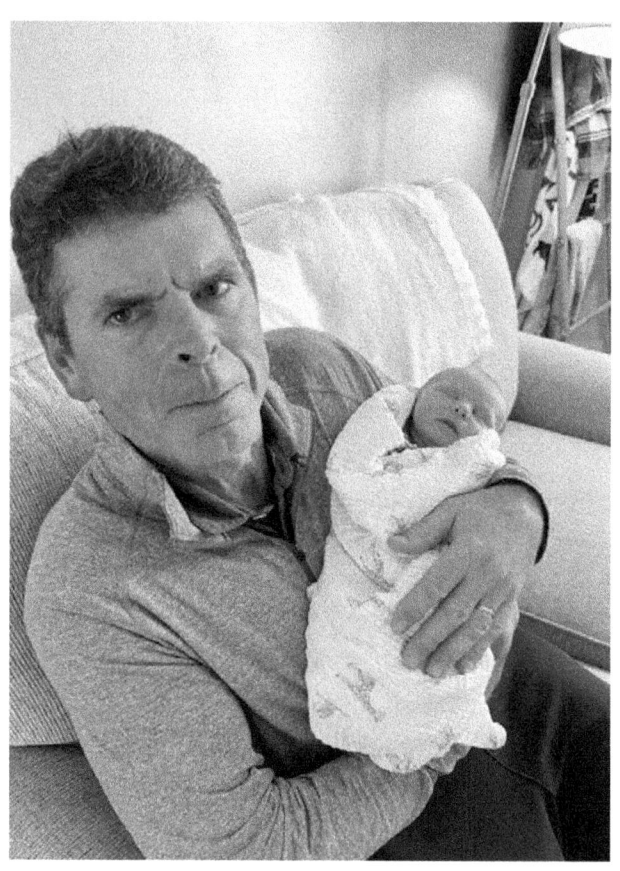

Grandpa and Owen

Now that we have a grandson, we just need a granddaughter to make this picture somewhat complete. Well, guess what? Bryce and Rachel welcomed their daughter, Palmer June Kelley, to the world on August 27th, 2024. If I had to describe her in one word—Angelic!

Baby Palmer and her Dad

As new grandparents, we hope that we have modeled appropriate behavior in being a responsible mom and dad. New moms and dads are not provided with a step-by-step manual on how to be the best parent. If a manual were to be created, I would hope that chapter one would thoroughly describe the importance of giving your children unlimited time and love.

While writing this book, we have accomplished many things, including my promise to those who like to hear funny and emotional student stories. I shared my experience having Parkinson's Disease. Also, I tried to give you the feeling of living in poverty.

This wraps up *We are Family*. You can use this document for fun and also as a serious document for future generations of the Kelley Family. Since we started writing *We Are Family*, we have lost two family members. My oldest brother Pat died on March 7, 2022. My mom died on January 13, 2023. They are missed!

Marcia—Mom

Patrick Kelley—Big Brother

In addition to celebrating the lives of mom and Patrick, we also celebrate the two, new family members—Owen Kelley (parents are Reid and Aubri) and baby girl Kelley due in August (parents are Bryce and Rachel). Also, my niece Shannon (daughter of Michael and Amy) and her husband Mitchell had their second child, James Patrick, in April.

From the youngest to the oldest members, we are all here for each other. Reflecting on our family, I think it's healthy for us to want to share stories about those who are not here anymore—including mom, Pat, and all of us that follow.

Life Lesson 7: Shortly after being diagnosed with Parkinson's, I traveled to Yale to participate in a research study. The first doctor I met with offered the following advice to my wife and me: "Both of you should quit your jobs and travel." Now if we were in our 80s, maybe that would have been appropriate. However, being thirty-five years old and having three young children, some better advice would have been: "We are going to fight, fight, fight together and we are going to beat this disease."

WE ARE FAMILY!

George Bailey

I was thirty-four years old with a young family,
a new job, why me?
I exercised every day, ate right, had strong
faith, what could it be?
I went to Chicago to get some answers to the
problems I had been facing
Dr. Goetz gave me the diagnosis of
Parkinson's, my heart started racing?

On great days I have no falls, no tremor, clear
thoughts and not asking "why me"
On good days I have some falls, no sleep,
tremors, and when walking must rest on one
knee
I don't want to be called a complainer or be a
burden, so I say there are no days that are bad.
The truth is there are some terrible times, but I
don't want the kids to worry about their dad

Now it's time to go to battle, you better not
bet against me,
I have teammates like Michael J. Fox, Kirk
Gibson, and family of Muhammed Ali.
My concern is for family, I don't want
worrying from my sons and wife
You can call me George Bailey, because it will
still be a wonderful life.

Chapter 7—Final Comments

Louie, an important member of our family, is checking out the morning sunrise on Blossom Trail. It's a new day for all of us, with so many possibilities— make the most of it!

The two newest members of the family are Owen and Palmer. In a word, they are "perfect". They give us hope for the future. Additionally, they will require Jody and me to be actively involved in school and community events and other happenings.

WE ARE FAMILY!

www.ingramcontent.com/pod-product-compliance
Lightning Source LLC
Chambersburg PA
CBHW051225120626
46547CB00013B/1509